Zoom In on

First Ladies

Eleanor Roosevelt

Jennifer Strand

abdopublishing.com

Published by Abdo Zoom™, PO Box 398166, Minneapolis, Minnesota 55439. Abdo Zoom™ is a trademark and logo of Abdo Consulting Group, Inc.

Printed in the United States of America, North Mankato, Minnesota
052017
092017

THIS BOOK CONTAINS
RECYCLED MATERIALS

Cover Photo: AP Images
Interior Photos: John Lent/AP Images, 4; Franklin D. Roosevelt Presidential Library & Museum, 5, 6, 7, 8, 13, 15, 18, 19; Library of Congress/Wikimedia, 9; Architect of the Capitol/Library of Congress, 10; Harris & Ewing/Library of Congress, 11, 14; Murray Becker/AP Images, 12; Elias Goldensky/Library of Congress, 16; Gerard Yvon Cheynet/AP Images, 17

Editor: Emily Temple
Series Designer: Madeline Berger
Art Direction: Dorothy Toth

Publisher's Cataloging-in-Publication Data
Names: Strand, Jennifer, author.
Title: Eleanor Roosevelt / by Jennifer Strand.
Description: Minneapolis, MN : Abdo Zoom, 2018. | Series: First ladies | Includes bibliographical references and index.
Identifiers: LCCN 2017931135 | ISBN 9781532120190 (lib. bdg.) | ISBN 9781614797302 (ebook) | 9781614797869 (Read-to-me ebook)
Subjects: LCSH: Roosevelt, Eleanor, 1884-1962--Juvenile literature. | Presidents spouses--United States--Biography--Juvenile literature.
Classification: DDC 973.917/092 [B]--dc23
LC record available at http://lccn.loc.gov/2017931135

Table of Contents

Introduction

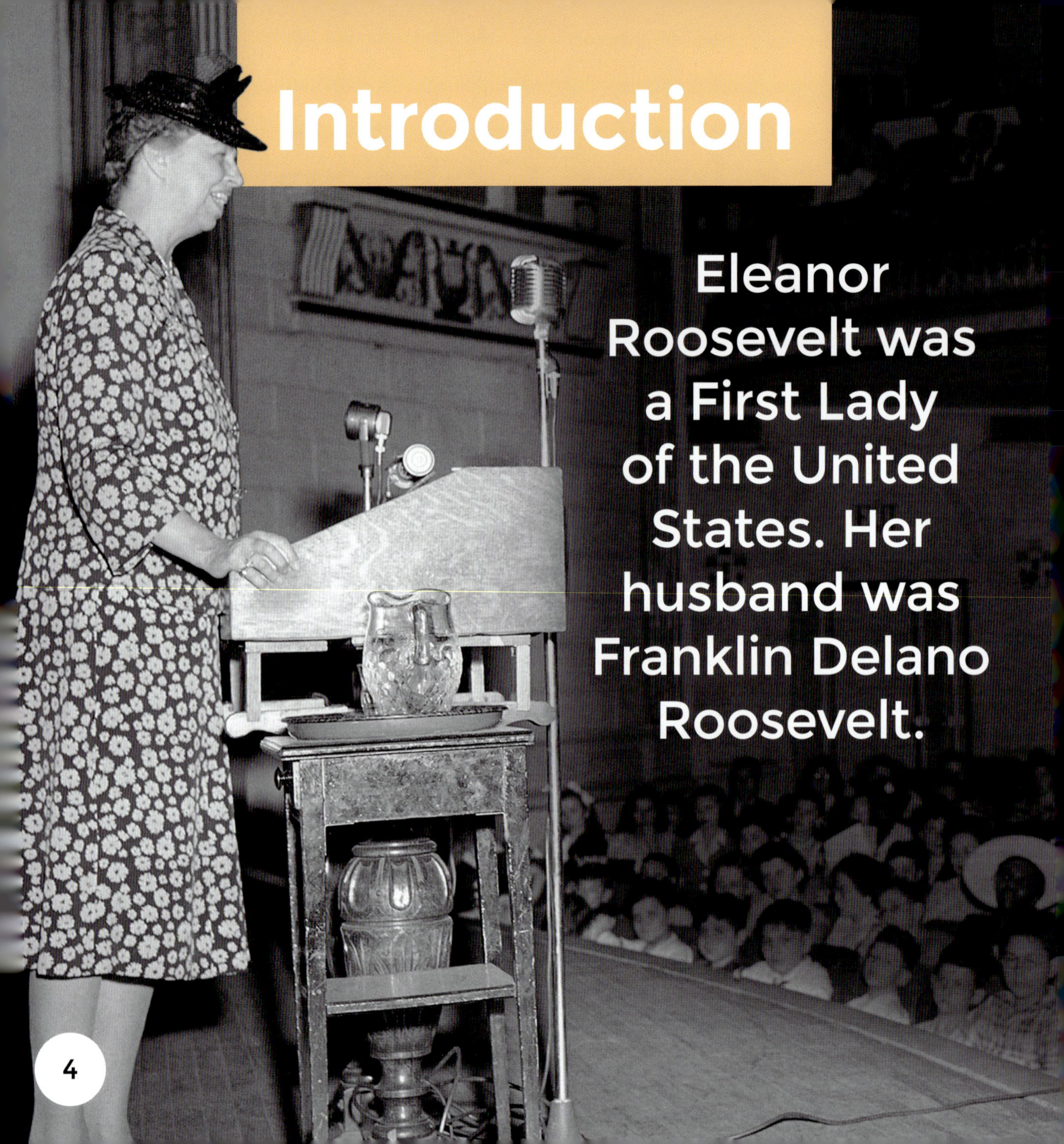

Eleanor Roosevelt was a First Lady of the United States. Her husband was Franklin Delano Roosevelt.

Eleanor fought for equal **rights**.
Her speeches and writings
are well known.

Early Life

Eleanor was born
on October 11, 1884.

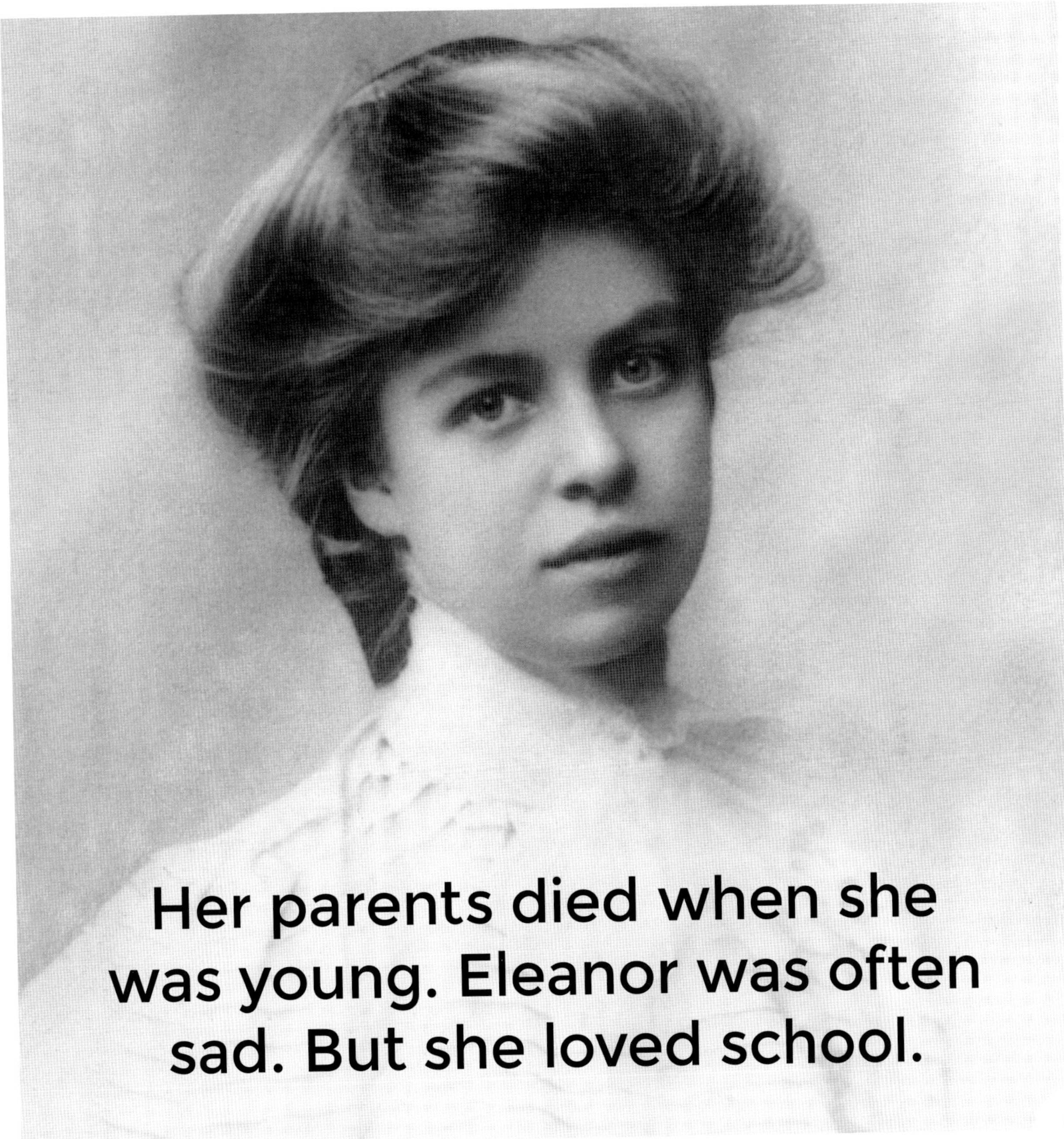

Her parents died when she was young. Eleanor was often sad. But she loved school.

Leader

In 1905 Eleanor married Franklin D. Roosevelt. She helped him with his jobs in **politics**.

Eleanor also worked to help people. She **volunteered** and worked as a teacher.

First Lady

Eleanor became First Lady of the United States in 1933.

She brought attention to important issues. She also wrote for newspapers.

Eleanor gave speeches, too. She spoke out against **racism**.

She also worked to help women and workers.

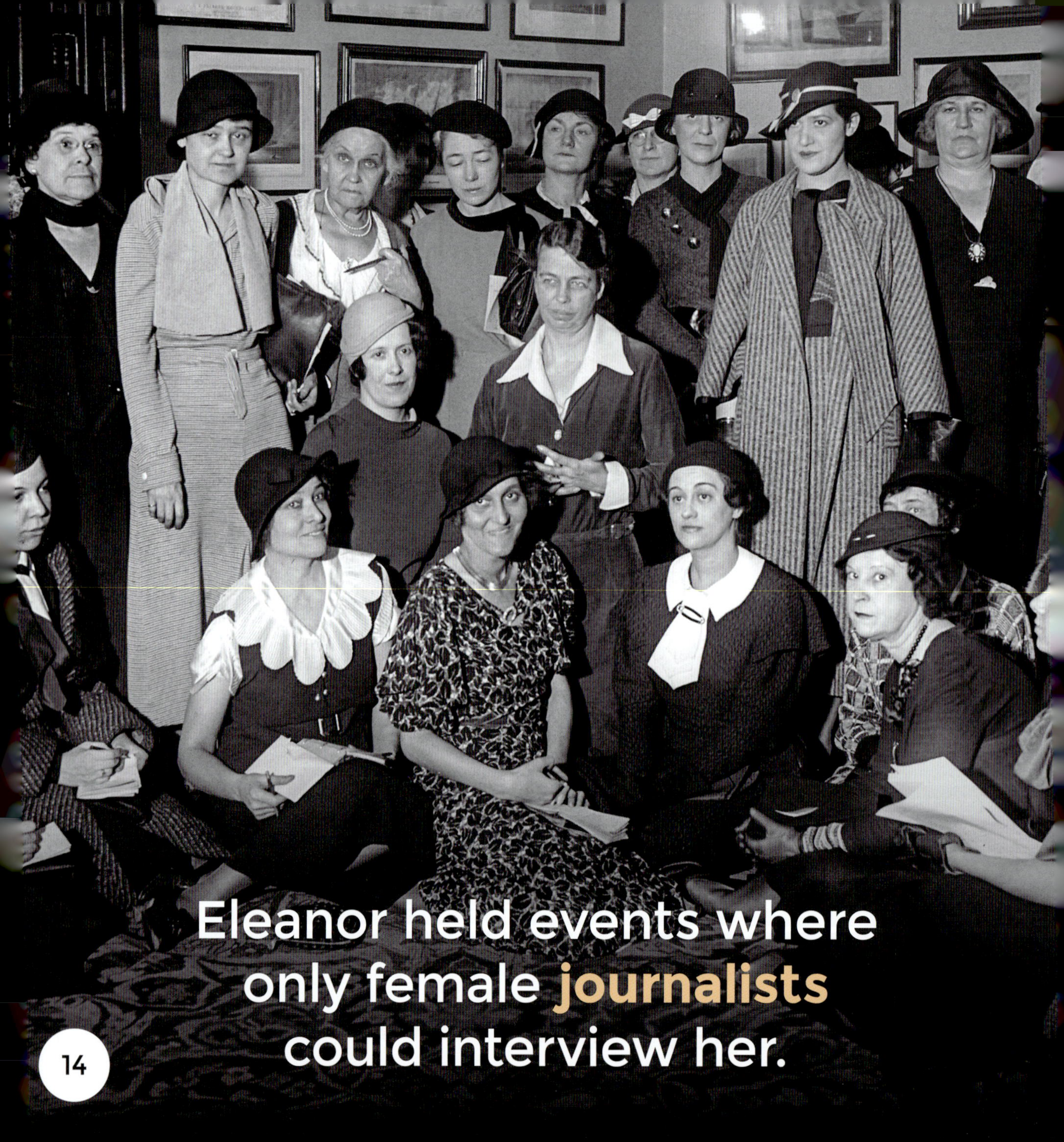

Eleanor held events where only female **journalists** could interview her.

As a result, newspapers hired more women.

Legacy

Franklin D. Roosevelt died in 1945.

Eleanor continued her work helping people gain equal rights.

On November 7, 1962, Eleanor died. Her ideas had not always been popular.

But she changed the way First Ladies acted. She showed they could speak out for change.

Quick Stats

Eleanor Roosevelt

Born: October 11, 1884

Birthplace: New York, New York

Husband: Franklin D. Roosevelt

Years Served: 1933–1945

Known For: Eleanor Roosevelt was a US First Lady, a civil rights activist, women's rights activist, and writer.

Died: November 7, 1962

Key Dates

1884: Anna Eleanor Roosevelt is born on October 11.

1905: Franklin D. Roosevelt and Eleanor are married on March 17.

1933–1945: Franklin D. Roosevelt is the 32nd US president. Eleanor Roosevelt is First Lady.

1945: Eleanor begins working for the United Nations.

1948: Eleanor helps write a document about human rights.

1962: Eleanor dies on November 7.

Glossary

journalist - a writer that gathers news.

politics - jobs and actions that keep the government running.

racism - treating someone poorly or taking away their rights because of the color of their skin.

rights - things that people are entitled to do under the law.

volunteer - to give time to help others without being paid.

Booklinks

For more information on **Eleanor Roosevelt**, please visit abdobooklinks.com

Zoom In on Biographies!

Learn even more with the Abdo Zoom Biographies database. Check out **abdozoom.com** for more information.

Index